Summer at Notforgotten Farm

Needlework Projects Inspired by Simple, Old-Fashioned Summer Days

By Lori Brechlin

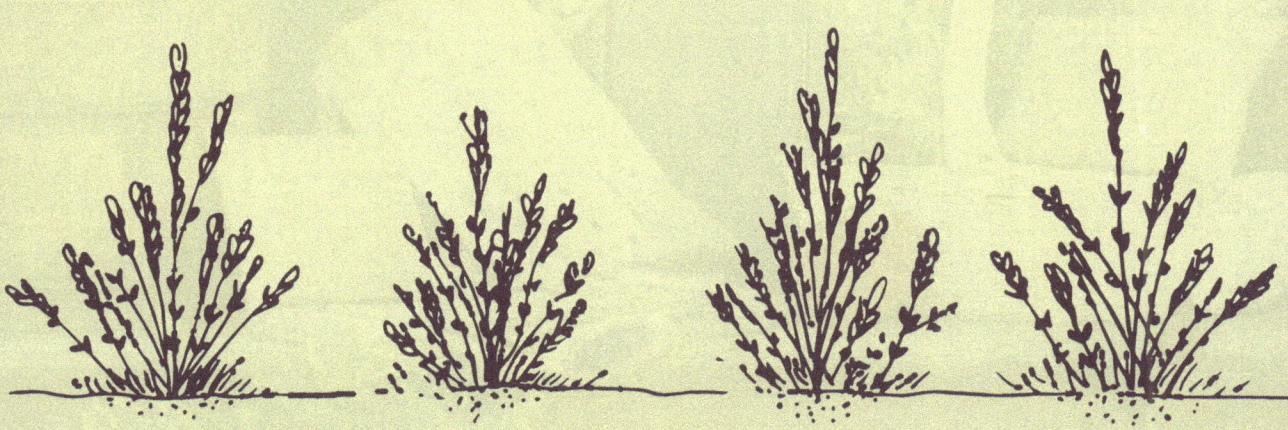

Lavender

Summer at Notforgotten Farm
Needlework Projects Inspired by Simple, Old-Fashioned Summer Days
By Lori Brechlin

Editor: Jenifer Dick
Designer: Sarah Mosher
Photography: Natalie Turley
Technical Editor: Mary Atherton

Published by:
Kansas City Star Books
1729 Grand Blvd.
Kansas City, Missouri, USA 64108

All rights reserved
Copyright © 2014 Lori Brechlin and The Kansas City Star Co.

No part of this book may be reproduced, stored in a retrieval system, or transmitted in any form or by any means, electronic, mechanical, photocopying, recording or otherwise, without the prior consent of the publisher.

No finished projects featured in this book can be produced or sold commercially without the permission of the author and publisher.

POD Edition
ISBN: 978-1-61169-125-2

Library of Congress Control Number: 2014934279

Kansas City Star Quilts is an imprint of C&T Publishing, Inc., P.O. Box 1456, Lafayette, CA 94549. ctpub.com

Photos for "Summer at Notforgotten Farm" were taken by Natalie Turley Photography at Notforgotten Farm, Amherst, Va.

Contents

4 Acknowledgments

5 Introduction

8 Basic Instructions

11 Supplies

The Projects

12 Summer Farmhouse Sampler

18 Lavender and Rosemary Pillows

22 Garden Basket Hanger

26 Summer Banner

30 Tomato Needle Minder

34 Seeds Pocket

38 Lavender Basket Chair Pad

46 Cherry Tomato Pinkeep Necklace

48 About the Author

Dedication

To those who work with their hearts and hands creating beautiful, simple things.

Acknowledgments

Having the opportunity to work once again with the wonderful folks at Kansas City Star Books is a dream come true. I am so very thankful for your support and faith in me.

To Peter — thank you for the constant flow of positive energy, the countless words of encouragement and the continuous cups of tea. You hold my heart.

To Hannah — you have been my strength from day one. I am the luckiest mother in the world. I love you so very much.

To Mom — I am so proud to be your daughter. Your encouraging words, patience and support allow me to follow my dreams. I love you more than all the little blue flowers on the wallpaper!

To Louisea and Sharon, my sisters and best friends — having the two of you in my life is more than a sister could ever hope for. I love you both dearly.

To Joan and Felicia — I am blessed beyond measure to have you by my side. I admire your strength in putting up with me and hope you never stop. Thank you for the friendship … xoxox.

Introduction

The summer months spent at Notforgotten Farm are peaceful and slow — waking to the sound of our beloved roosters and quietly sipping tea on our front porch is inspiration enough for my needlework. Quiet hours spent in the gardens encourage my thoughts to wander to my waiting needle and thread, where I can incorporate the colors and textures of my plantings with my wools, cotton fabrics and linen.

Finding time to do a little handwork after the daily chores is something I look forward to each day, but especially on a bright and sunny summer afternoon, sitting close to the lavender bushes and watching the honeybees dance on the tops of the fresh herbs. Making time everyday to connect with nature and enjoy my creating is very important to me.

The projects in this book are inspired by my gardens. The sights, sounds and colors of my herbs and flowers find their way into my handwork. I hope you enjoy your visit here with me.

Inspiration for the **Lavender Basket** hooked wool chair pad comes from enjoying the harvesting of our lavender in the early summer — its colors are deep and rich, like the scent of lavender.

The **Rosemary and Lavender** cross-stitched pillows are perfect to hold your needles and pins — but they can also be filled with dried herbs and used as sachets.

The **Summer Farmhouse Sampler** cross stitch is mounted in an antique frame — one that is reminiscent of the time period of this humble farmhouse. The colors used in the sampler are pulled from my memories of bright, sunny days spent working in the garden.

Garden Basket Hanger punch needle is a small project that can be hung on a cupboard door or basket. Its simple design is quick and easy to work on in between other larger projects.

The **Seeds Pocket** appliqué is made from scraps of an old feed sack and new, but vintage-looking, cotton calico fabrics. Use this to keep your seeds for planting next year or a small needlework project.

Tomato Needle Minder is a sweet way to keep those stray pins in reach. The deep red colors and floss shading replicate a delicious, garden-ripe delight!

The **Summer Banner** is a fun way to decorate for the season. Hang yours from the garden gate or trellis to celebrate those breezy summer days.

Cherry Tomato Pinkeep Necklace — a small token to wear while you stitch — is made from scraps of leftover fabric from your larger projects. It is a tiny reminder of gifts from the garden.

Remember to take time for yourself and your handwork. Enjoy the process of gathering your supplies and notions. Find a quiet place where you can enjoy the sun on your face and a gentle breeze while you work on these projects. A nice, tall glass of iced mint tea, a few chirping birds and you'll transport yourself back to a simpler time once again — back to a summer at Notforgotten Farm.

Basic Instructions

The projects in this book were designed assuming the reader has basic knowledge of rug hooking, appliqué, counted cross stitch, hand sewing and punch needle. Here are a few things I do that may help you to achieve an old, faded, vintage look to your finished projects.

AGING COTTON FABRIC

I hand wash all of my cotton fabric in hot water, using mild dish soap and a cool rinse. Once it has been rinsed well, I hang it outdoors on a line in full sun to help fade it a bit. I will generally wash a bunch of fat quarters at one time, and hang them all on the line for a couple of days. The sun fades them nicely, and they become so very soft to work with.

Once the fabric has dried and faded, I use a fine grit sandpaper to age the fabric a little more. Do this by gently rubbing in spots, being careful not to tear your fabric. After sanding the fabric, I stain it using a weak bath of coffee, tea or walnut stain. This lends an aged mellow look to my fabric.

To stain the fabric, place an old, cotton towel on your work surface. Place your cotton fabric, facing up, on the towel. Then use an old bristle paintbrush and dip it into the stain or dye bath. Next, brush the stain onto the fabric in random places where you want the staining to occur.

I do not like to dip my whole fabric directly into the stain or dye because I like the look of random staining – like a true, actual stain from long ago. I dry my stained fabric in the sun or in the oven on a cookie sheet on low heat. The heat causes the tannins in the stain or dye to darken. You can reapply more stain to darken it as you wish.

HAND STITCHING

I prefer to hand stitch my work, but will turn to my sewing machine for larger work, such as piecing or quilting.

I use plain cotton thread in a brown, natural or linen color. I use simple embroidery needles because of their larger eyes (easier for my eyes to thread!), and I never worry about the size of my stitches or if they're "perfect." Worrying about perfection in my handwork causes stress, and I don't enjoy stress!

Instead of using perle cottons or heavier threads for appliqué, I prefer to use cotton thread. I just simply stitch around my appliqué pieces with a primitive whip stitch. I like the look this lends to my simple designs.

RUG HOOKING

I pull wool loops through a linen backing. It's really that simple! There is no mystery to rug hooking, no "secret" techniques. My loops are not even and my wool strips are not all the same width because I choose to hand cut them using my Fiskars spring-loaded scissors. I recycle wool skirts and clothing from thrift stores, and I love the wools offered on the market that are especially milled for rug hooking – hand dyed or as-is.

I love to use an antique rug hook that I have had for many years. It has a very sharp hook and large ferrule to open my linen backing to accommodate my wool strips. You can find many rug hooks by visiting shops online that sell rug hooking supplies.

PUNCH NEEDLE

Punch needle is a very rewarding form of embroidery that mimics the look of a hooked rug. It is inexpensive, portable and fun to do! Punch needle takes a bit of practice, but you will love it once you master it.

Cross Stitch

CROSS STITCH

My technique for counted cross stitch may differ a bit from yours. I was taught to find the center of my design and begin stitching there. I have difficulty in judging linen sizes using this technique, and not being one to waste anything (especially linen!), I found a better way for me. I find it much easier to begin my stitching in either the upper left or lower left corner of the design and work my way out from there. If there is a border, I begin stitching at the upper or lower left and then complete the border. Then I move on to the designs, motifs, letters, numerals, etc.

My designs for cross stitch are stitched on linen, using 1 strand of floss over 2 threads of linen. I prefer working with and using DMC floss — it is inexpensive, found at almost every hobby, craft or needlework store and is dye-fast. Since I love to stain my finished cross-stitched projects, using dye-fast floss is very important to me.

When I do use hand-dyed floss, Gentle Arts Threads and Weeks Dye Works threads are my choices.

Please remember these are just guidelines. I'm happy to share my way of doing things, but if you find your way easier, stick to what you like!

I am always available to answer any of your questions or to hear your comments or concerns regarding the basic instructions above — you may contact me via email at **not4got@aol.com**.

SUMMER AT NOTFORGOTTEN FARM

Supplies

SUPPLIES FOR THE PROJECTS IN THIS BOOK CAN BE FOUND AT THESE SHOPS:

CROSS STITCH, PUNCH NEEDLE AND RUG HOOKING SUPPLIES, AND ORGANIC SAWDUST:

Notforgotten Farm
3530 Tye River Road
Amherst, VA 24521
Phone: (434) 263-6508
Email: not4got@aol.com
www.farmhousenotforgotten.blogspot.com
www.notforgottenfarm.etsy.com

COTTON FABRICS:

Cottonwood Quilt Shop
2035 Barracks Road
Charlottesville, VA 22903
Phone: (434) 244-9975

ANTIQUES SHOPS FOR FABRIC, NOTIONS, ETC.:

Appomattox Gallery
1850 Church Street
Appomattox, VA 24522
Phone: (434) 352-9590
www.appomattoxgallery.com

The Factory Antique Mall
50 Lodge Lane Suite 106
Verona, VA 24482
Phone: (540) 248-1110
www.factoryantiquemall.com

HAND-DYED WOOL:

Blackberry Primitives
Email: wool@blackberryprimitives.com
www.blackberryprimitives.com

FLOSS:

DMC Corporation — 6 Strand Cotton Floss
www.dmc-usa.com

SCISSORS:

Fiskars spring-loaded scissors
www.fiskars.com

COATS & CLARK COTTON QUILTING AND SEWING THREAD:

Jo-Ann Stores
www.joann.com

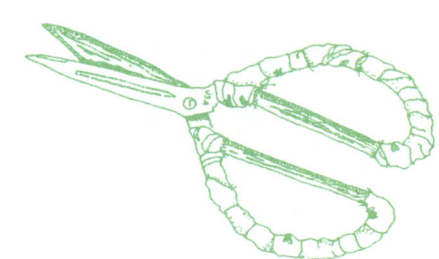

CROSS STITCH

Summer Farmhouse Sampler

Designed and Framed by Lori Brechlin

Stitched by Felicia Martin

Finished Size: 8⅞" × 11"

Stitch Count: 133W × 165H

NEEDFULS

16" × 18" piece of 30ct. Old Farmhouse Linen from Notforgotten Farm (see supplies page)

Wooden frame with an 11" × 13" opening

2 pieces of 11" × 13" cardboard to fit the frame opening

Elmer's brand spray adhesive

Hammer and small nails

Symbols   DMC Floss

1 skein each:

Symbol	DMC	Color
2	3852	straw — very dark
3	730	olive green — very dark
5	829	golden olive — very dark
8	400	mahogany — dark
◼	975	golden brown — dark
✖	3740	antique violet — dark
♣	781	topaz — very dark
★	3826	golden brown

INSTRUCTIONS

The charts are on pages 14–17.

Cross stitch with 1 strand of floss over 2 threads of linen using charted directions.

Finishing

Cut the cardboard to the opening dimension of the frame. Spray a light coat of spray adhesive on 1 piece of the cardboard. Once it's tacky, lay your finished project on the cardboard, centering the sampler evenly. Place the project in the frame. Lay the second piece of cardboard on the backside of the frame and, using small nails, tack the cardboard securely into place.

I used a beautiful antique frame that I found while out antiquing with friends. It was the perfect choice for this sampler! If you prefer, you can have your project framed professionally at reasonable prices at any local hobby/craft store in your area.

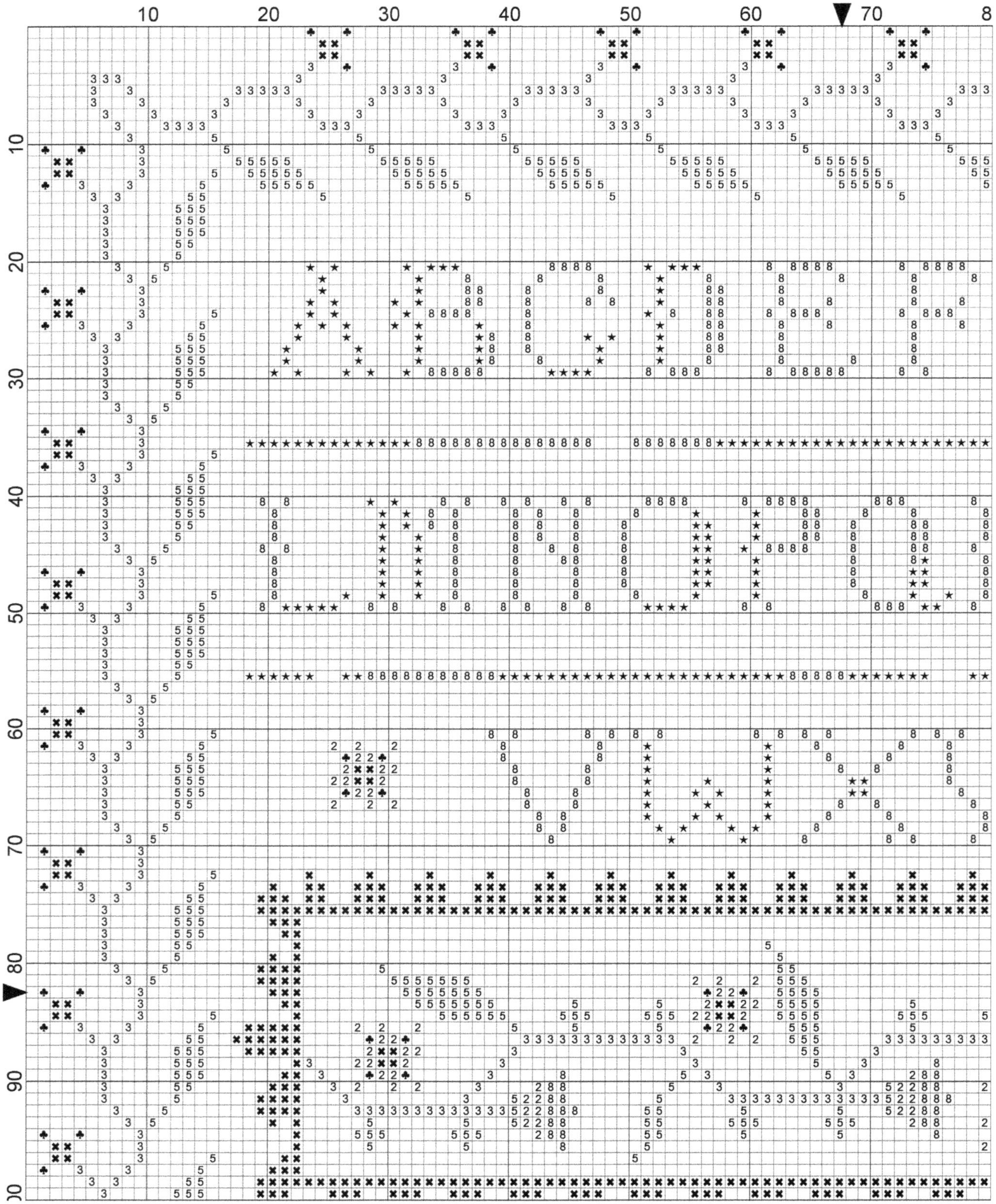

SUMMER AT NOTFORGOTTEN FARM

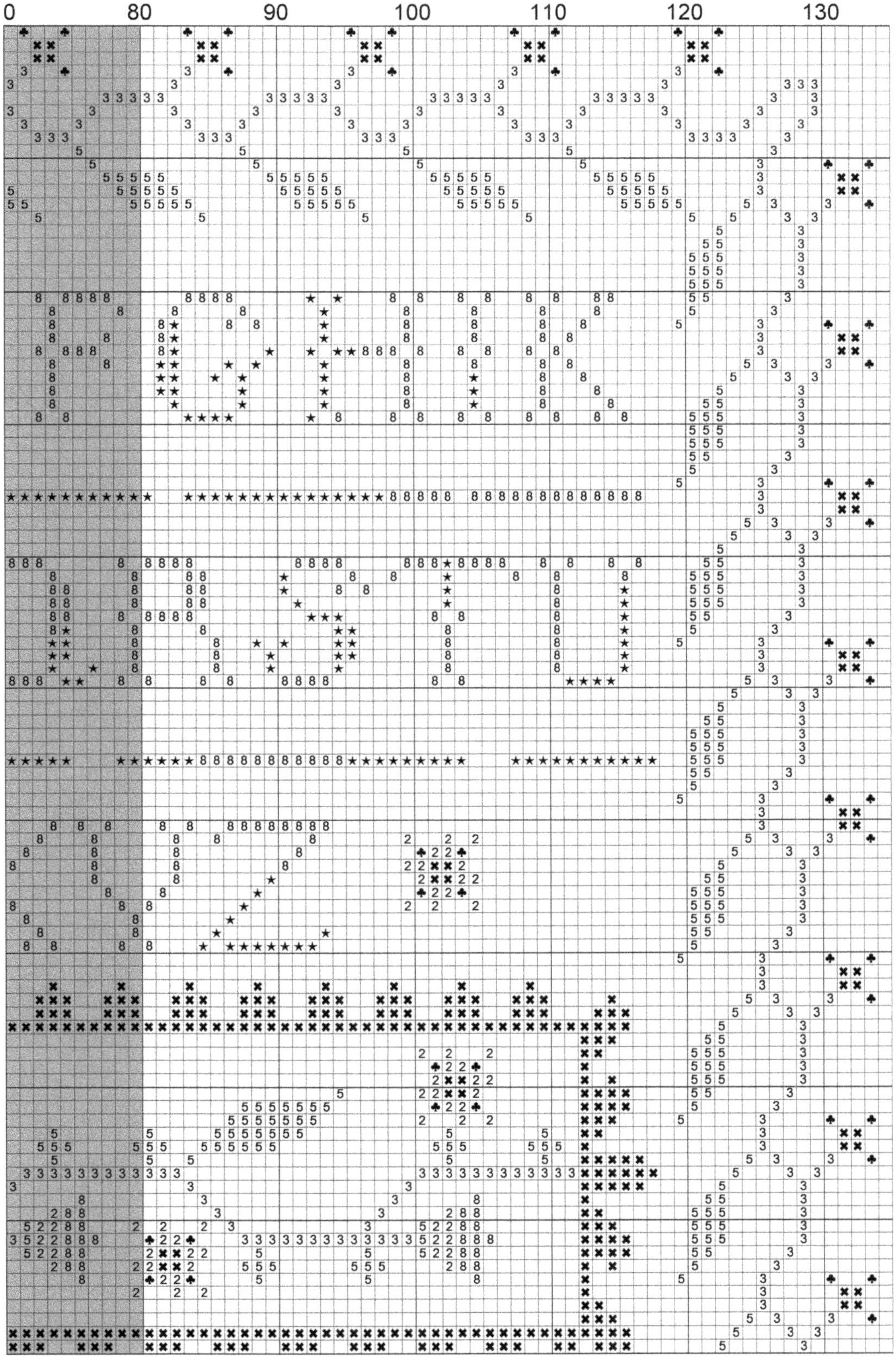

gray indicates repeat

SUMMER FARMHOUSE SAMPLER

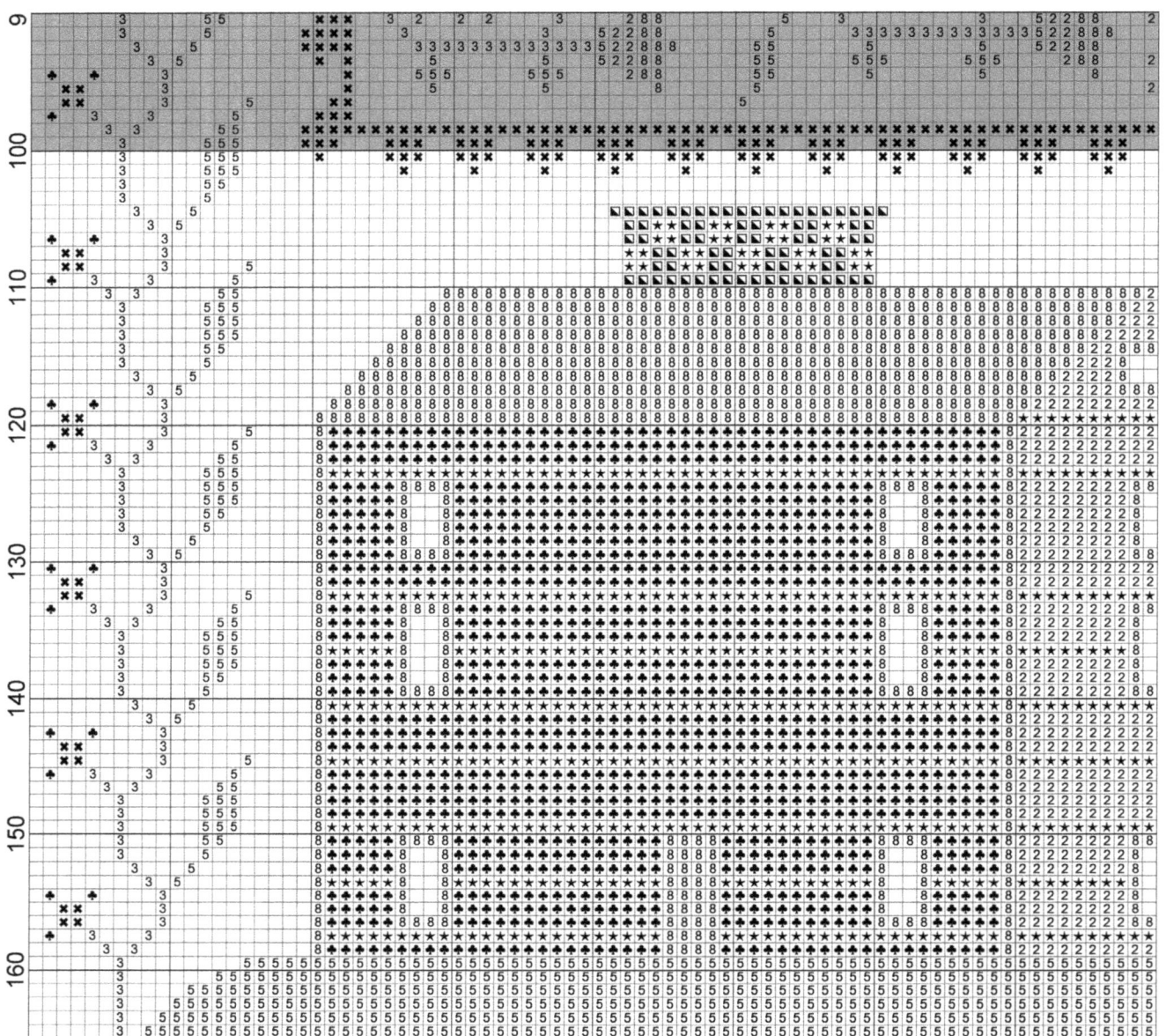

SUMMER AT NOTFORGOTTEN FARM

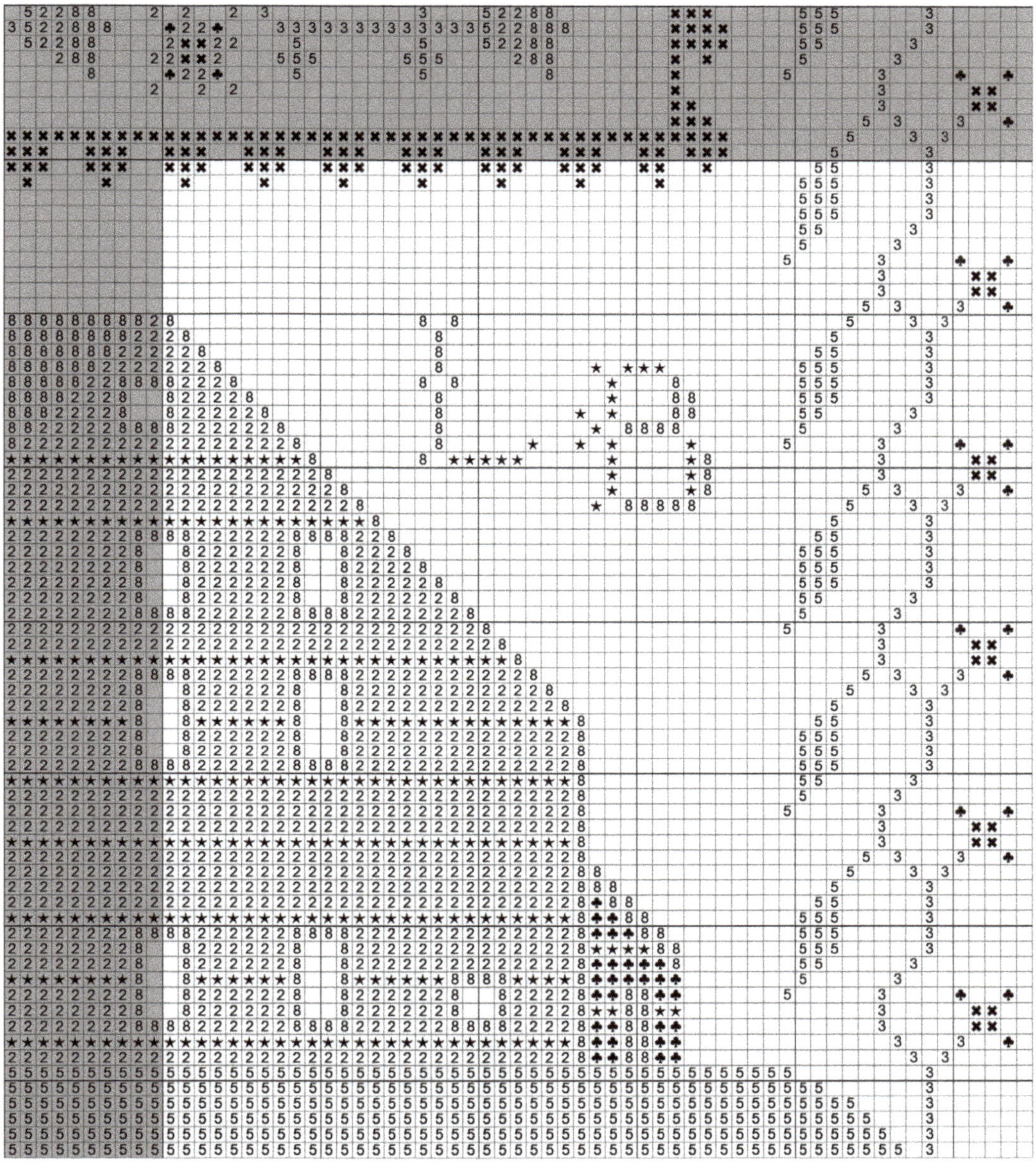

gray indicates repeat

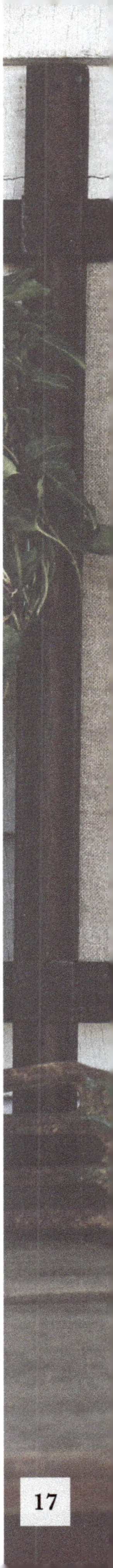

SUMMER FARMHOUSE SAMPLER

CROSS STITCH

Lavender and Rosemary Pillows

Designed and Finished by Lori Brechlin

Stitched by Felicia Martin

Finished Size: 7" × 5" each

Stitch Count: 105W × 75H each

NEEDFULS FOR EACH PILLOW

7" × 9" piece of 30ct. Old Farmhouse Linen from Notforgotten Farm (see supplies page)

7" × 9" piece of cotton fabric for backing

Needle, thread, scissors

Organic sawdust for stuffing (or dried herbs)

SUMMER AT NOTFORGOTTEN FARM

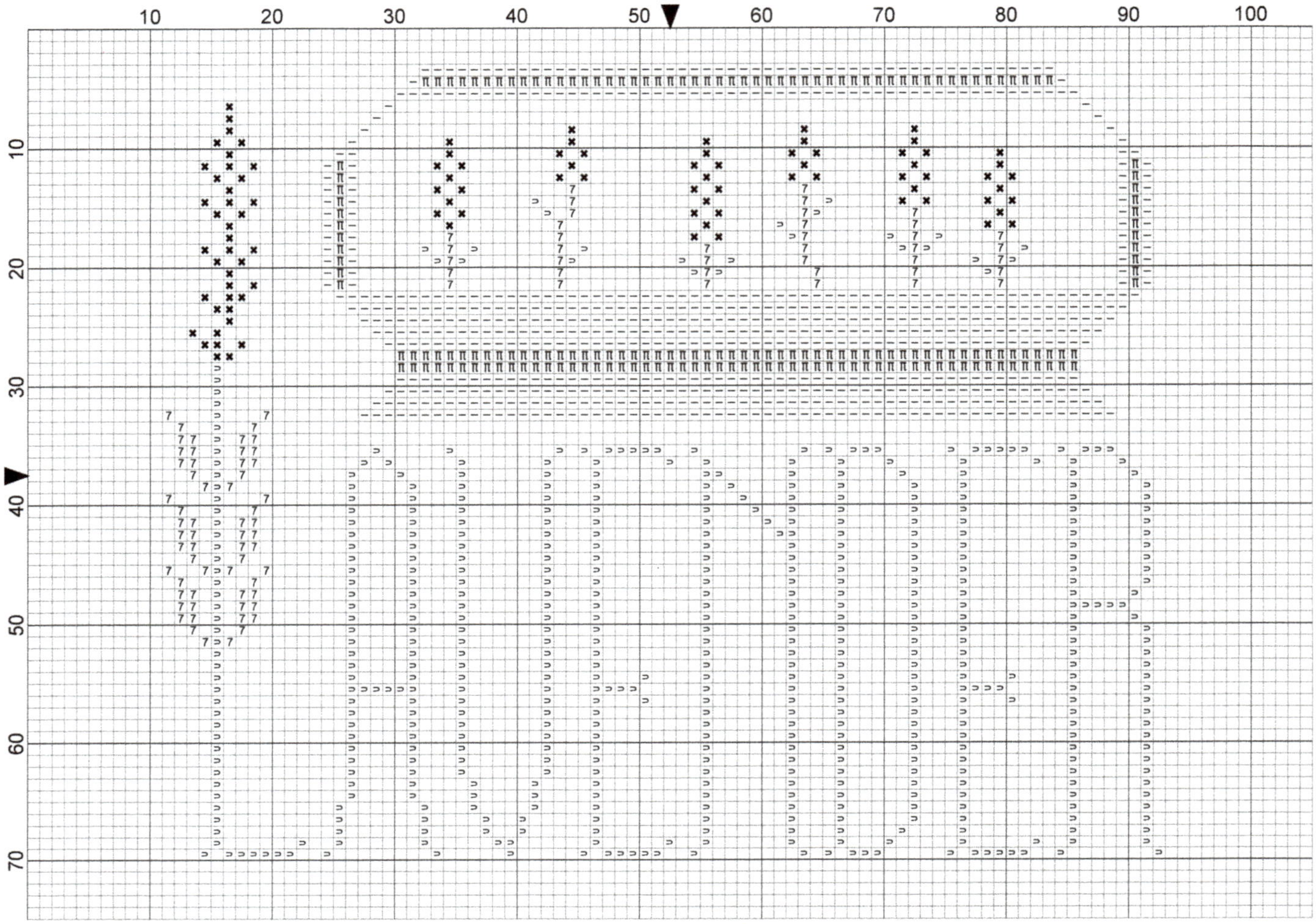

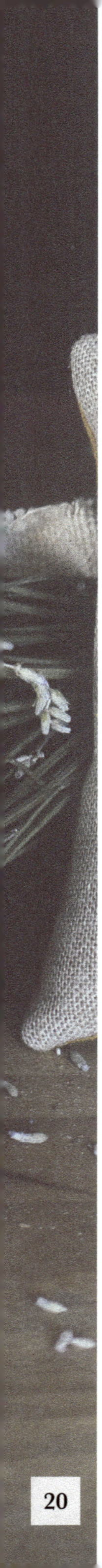

LAVENDER PILLOW
Symbols   DMC Floss

1 skein each:

Symbol	DMC	Color
–	611	drab brown
⊃	831	golden olive — medium
π	3033	mocha brown — very light
7	733	olive green — medium
✖	3740	antique violet — dark

ROSEMARY PILLOW
Symbols   DMC Floss

1 skein each:

Symbol	DMC	Color
–	611	drab brown
⊃	831	golden olive — medium
π	3033	mocha brown — very light
7	733	olive green — medium

SUMMER AT NOTFORGOTTEN FARM

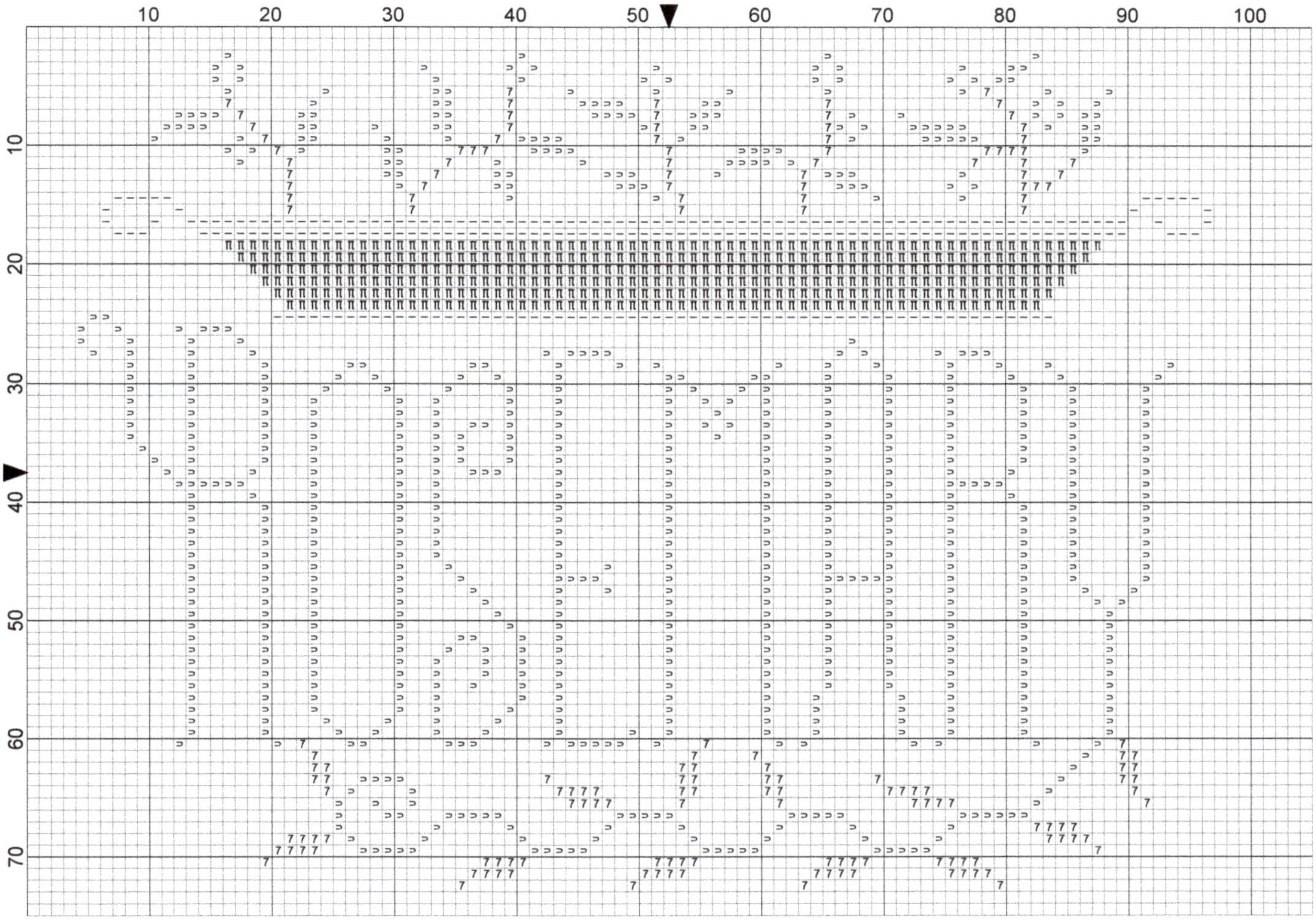

INSTRUCTIONS

Cross stitch each design with 1 strand of floss over 2 threads of linen using charted directions.

Finishing

Press the finished cross stitch from the backside, and lay it face down on your work surface. Using a pencil and ruler, draw a line 1" from the cross stitch on all 4 sides.

Lay the cotton backing fabric face up on the work surface, and lay the finished project face down, centering on top of the cotton.

Pin together the project and the cotton fabric, and sew on the drawn line all the way around. After sewing, cut away the excess linen and fabric, leaving a ¼" seam allowance around the stitched line.

Cut a 4" slit in the backing fabric, being careful not to cut the front cross stitch, and turn right sides out. Firmly stuff with sawdust, making sure to stuff each corner as well. Hand stitch the opening closed using cotton thread, and stitch on a small patch to hide the seam.

LAVENDER AND ROSEMARY PILLOWS

PUNCH NEEDLE

Garden Basket Hanger

Designed and Made by Lori Brechlin

Finished Size: 2 ½" × 6 ⅝" (not including hanger)

NEEDFULS

1 fat quarter of weavers cloth in white

3" × 8" piece of cotton fabric for backing

Lip lock hoop or gripper frame

Cameo Ultra Punch needle with medium tip

Sewing needle, cotton thread, small sharp scissors

9" piece of rusty wire (for hanger)

DMC Floss

1 skein 831 for lettering and border

1 skein 732 for stems

1 skein 733 for leaves

1 skein 3740 for lavender petals

1 skein 400 for red flowers

1 skein 3033 for background

4 skeins ecru for background

INSTRUCTIONS

The template is on page 24.

This design uses 6 strands of DMC floss throughout the entire design and a Cameo Ultrapunch needle with a medium tip set on the #2 setting.

Using the Garden Basket template, center and trace the design onto the weavers cloth with a pencil. Place the traced design into the lip lock hoop or on the gripper frame, centering the design and making sure the weavers cloth is drum-tight.

Punching the Design

Punch the design in the following order:

    831 for all lettering and border

    732 for all stems

    733 for all leaves

    3740 for all lavender petals

    400 for all red flowers

Fill in the background using the ecru floss, leaving some open spots. Fill the open spots with 3033.

SUMMER AT NOTFORGOTTEN FARM

Finishing

After the punching is complete, remove the project from the hoop or frame. Trim away any loose thread ends on the front (finished side) of the project.

Lay the cotton backing fabric face up on your work surface. Lay the finished project face down on top of that. Pin both the front and back fabrics together, and stitch completely around the entire project as close as you can to the last punched row. Trim away the excess fabric to within ¼" of the stitched row. Make a small slit in the center of the backing fabric being careful not to slit the project. Turn the project right sides out, and using a pencil, make sure the corners of the project are turned out fully.

Using a hot iron, gently press the finished project from the back. Stitch the slit closed using cotton thread, and cover the slit with a patch from a scrap.

Attach the rusty wire by poking through the end of the wire into both top corners of the project. Loop the wire at the ends.

SUMMER AT NOTFORGOTTEN FARM

PRIMITIVE STITCH

Summer Banner

Designed and Finished by Lori Brechlin
Finished Size: 46" long
Each Triangle: 5" × 6"

NEEDFULS

6 — 5½" × 6½" pieces of assorted vintage reproduction cotton print fabrics in varying shades of blue, brown, cream, green and lavender

6 — 5½" × 6½" pieces of Osnaburg fabric

1 — ¾" × 46" piece of vintage reproduction cotton print fabric in blue

DMC floss 831

Sewing needle, pins, cotton thread, paper, pencil and small sharp scissors

INSTRUCTIONS

Templates are on pages 28–29.

SUMMER AT NOTFORGOTTEN FAR

cut 5 from Osnaburg
cut 5 from asst'. cotton fabrics

Trace the triangle shape onto the paper, and cut out on the line. Then trace the triangle shape onto the Osnaburg fabric. Make 6.

Using the letter templates, trace each letter onto the Osnaburg triangles, being careful to place the penciled letter low on the triangle. (Refer to the photo for placement.)

Stitch the letters using 3 strands of floss in a primitive cross stitch.

Finishing

Lay the cotton fabric pieces face up on your work surface. Lay the stitched triangle pieces face down on them, and pin both the front and back fabrics together.

Stitch together following the penciled triangle line on both sides, leaving the top open to turn. Repeat for each letter. Once all triangles are stitched, trim away the excess fabric to within $1/4$" from the seam. Turn all of the triangles right sides out, and with a pencil, make sure the point of each triangle is turned out completely.

Place the 46"-long piece of fabric on your worktable. Place your stitched triangles on top of the fabric strip, placed evenly about $1\,3/4$" apart, with the tops of the triangles measuring approximately 1" covering the fabric strip from the top. Pin the triangles in place along the strip so they don't slide. Stitch each triangle to the fabric strip by hand or machine using cotton thread.

You can add more age to your finished banner by staining it with a little bit of tea or strong coffee and hanging it in the summer sun to dry. Our banner graces the front porch where it greets us each morning, reminding us to celebrate the season!

SUMMER BANNER

PUNCH NEEDLE

Tomato Needle Minder

Designed and Finished by Lori Brechlin

Finished size: 3½" × 4"

NEEDFULS

¼ yard weavers cloth in white

5" × 5" piece of red print cotton fabric

4" × 4" piece of faded, red-colored wool

Small white ring for hanging

Cameo Ultrapunch Needle with medium tip

Lip lock hoop or gripper frame

Sewing needle, thread, pins, small sharp scissors and pencil

DMC Floss

2 skeins 3826 for tomato

3 skeins 919 for tomato

1 skein 831 for leaves

1 skein 732 for leaves

INSTRUCTIONS

The template is on page 33.

Use 6 strands of DMC floss throughout the entire design and a Cameo Ultrapunch needle set on the #2 setting.

Trace the design onto the weavers cloth using a pencil, and place the traced project into the lip lock hoop or on gripper frame. Make sure the weavers cloth is drum-tight.

Punching the Design

Punch the design in the following order:

831 for leaf outlines, filling in the leaves with 732.

919 for tomato outlines and fill in, leaving some open spots. Fill in the open spots with 3826.

SUMMER AT NOTFORGOTTEN FARM

Finishing

After the punching is complete, remove the project from the hoop or frame. Trim away any loose threads from the front of the project.

Place the backing fabric face up on your work surface. Lay your punched project face down on top of that, and pin both the front and back fabrics together. Stitch completely around the entire finished project as close as you can to the last punched row. Trim away the excess weavers cloth and fabric to within $\frac{1}{4}$" of your stitched line.

Cut a small slit into the backing fabric in the center, being careful not to cut the loops on the front of the project. You may need to clip the edges and then turn the project right side out. Using the red wool and template, cut out a circle to cover the slit and whip stitch the wool patch into place using cotton thread. Stitch the small, white ring to the top of the tomato using cotton thread. Add a small thin strip of green wool (if desired) by tying it to the ring.

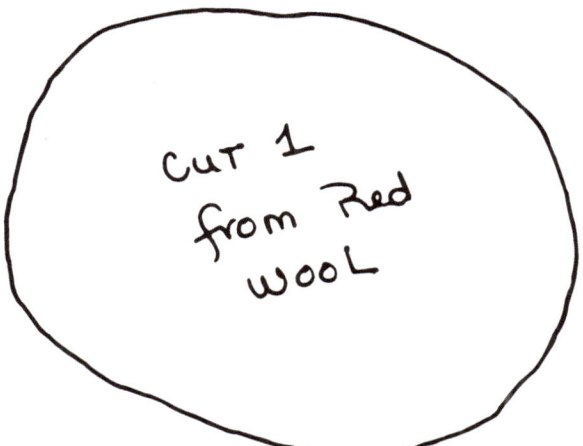

Cut 1 from Red Wool

TOMATO NEEDLE MINDER

APPLIQUÉ

Seeds Pocket

Designed and Finished by Lori Brechlin
Finished Project Size: 8" × 11"

NEEDFULS

5 — 3" × 4 ½" pieces of assorted cotton print fabrics (2 blue, 1 brown, 2 cream) for lettering

2 — 9" × 12" pieces of a vintage feedsack or light fabric for the pocket

1 — ½" × 36" strip of cotton fabric for the drawstring

DMC floss 3021

Fray check

Sewing needle, safety pin, cotton thread, pencil, paper and small, sharp scissors

INSTRUCTIONS

Appliqué

The templates are on page 36.

Begin by tracing the letters onto white paper using a pencil. Cut out the paper letter templates on the line, and pin to the right sides of the corresponding cotton fabric. Trace the letters onto the fabric, and cut out the letters. Apply the fray check to the raw edges of all the fabric letters, and let dry.

Place 1 of the 9" × 12" pocket fabrics onto your work surface. Pin the fabric letters into place within 1" from the bottom. Using the cotton thread and a needle, whip stitch the edges of the fabric letters onto the pocket fabric in a primitive manner.

Using 2 strands of the floss, primitively stitch the date "1896" where indicated using tiny cross stitches.

SUMMER AT NOTFORGOTTEN FARM

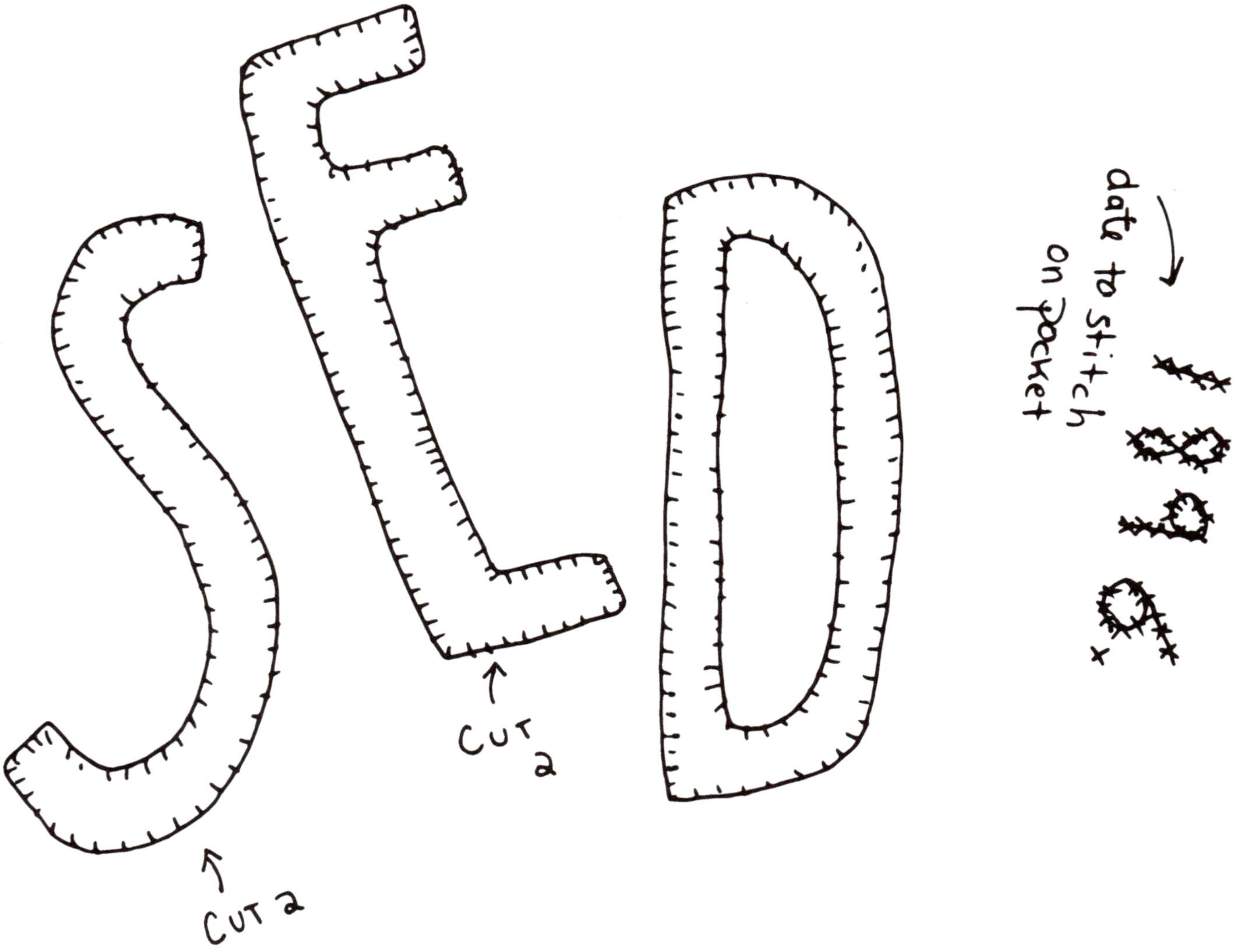

SED

← date to stitch on pocket

↑ CUT 2

↑ CUT 2

Finishing

Place the second piece of fabric on your work surface. Place the front of the pocket (with letters) face down onto that. Pin both the front and back of the project together, and machine or hand-stitch around both sides and the bottom of pocket, leaving the top open. Trim away the excess fabric to within ¼" at the stitched seams. Turn the pocket right sides out.

Turn the top of the pocket opening down inside the pocket ¼", and whip stitch the edge into place. Cut small slits into the pocket fabric just below the top hem to accommodate the fabric strip drawstring. Attach a safety pin to one end of the drawstring strip, and feed it through the slits in the pocket fabric, coming in and out of every other slit, and ending back where you began. Tie the drawstring strip ends together.

SUMMER AT NOTFORGOTTEN FARM

HOOKED WOOL

Lavender Basket Chair Pad

Designed and Made by Lori Brechlin
Finished Size: Approximately 13" Round

NEEDFULS

- ½ yard of linen, burlap or monk's cloth for the rug hooking foundation
- ⅛ yard of assorted purple wools for flowers and the scalloped border
- ⅛ yard of green wool for the stems
- ⅛ yard of greenish brown wool for the leaves
- ¼ yard of assorted brown wools for the basket
- ¼ yard of textured black and cream wool for the border and scallops
- ½ yard of assorted white wools for the background
- Red dot tracer tracing paper or pellon paper transfer fabric
- Black Sharpie marker
- Sharp scissors
- Rotary cutter or wool cutter and mat
- Large quilter's hoop or gripper rug frame
- Large needle and heavy white thread

SUMMER AT NOTFORGOTTEN FARM

INSTRUCTIONS

Hooking

The templates are on pages 42–45.

Trace the pattern onto your rug backing using a black marker and transfer fabric or paper. Make sure to leave at least 4" of foundation around the edge of the chair pad circle line.

Cut your wool into ¼" strips using a rotary cutter, scissors or wool cutter. Begin hooking the tops of the flowers first, then move onto the stems and leaves. Now hook the basket and handle. Next, hook the border and outline of the scallops along the border, then fill in the scallops. Last, fill in the entire background using the white wools.

Finishing

Once the hooking is completed, dampen a small towel with water and place it on top of the loops on your project. Using a hot iron, gently steam the project so the loops lay nicely. Let it dry completely if it gets damp.

Trim away the excess foundation around the entire design to within 1" of the last hooked row.

Fold the foundation fabric once toward the back. You may need to make small slits in the foundation to help it lay flat, but be careful not to slit too close to the hooked row. Turn back once more for a neat edge, and whipstitch the edge using the heavy white thread.

You can age your chair pad by brewing a cup of strong tea or coffee and dabbing it onto the loops, letting the stain seep in a bit. Let it dry outside in the full sun.

Make sure to stitch your name or initials onto the back of your work for future generations!

SUMMER AT NOTFORGOTTEN FARM

LAVENDER BASKET CHAIR PAD

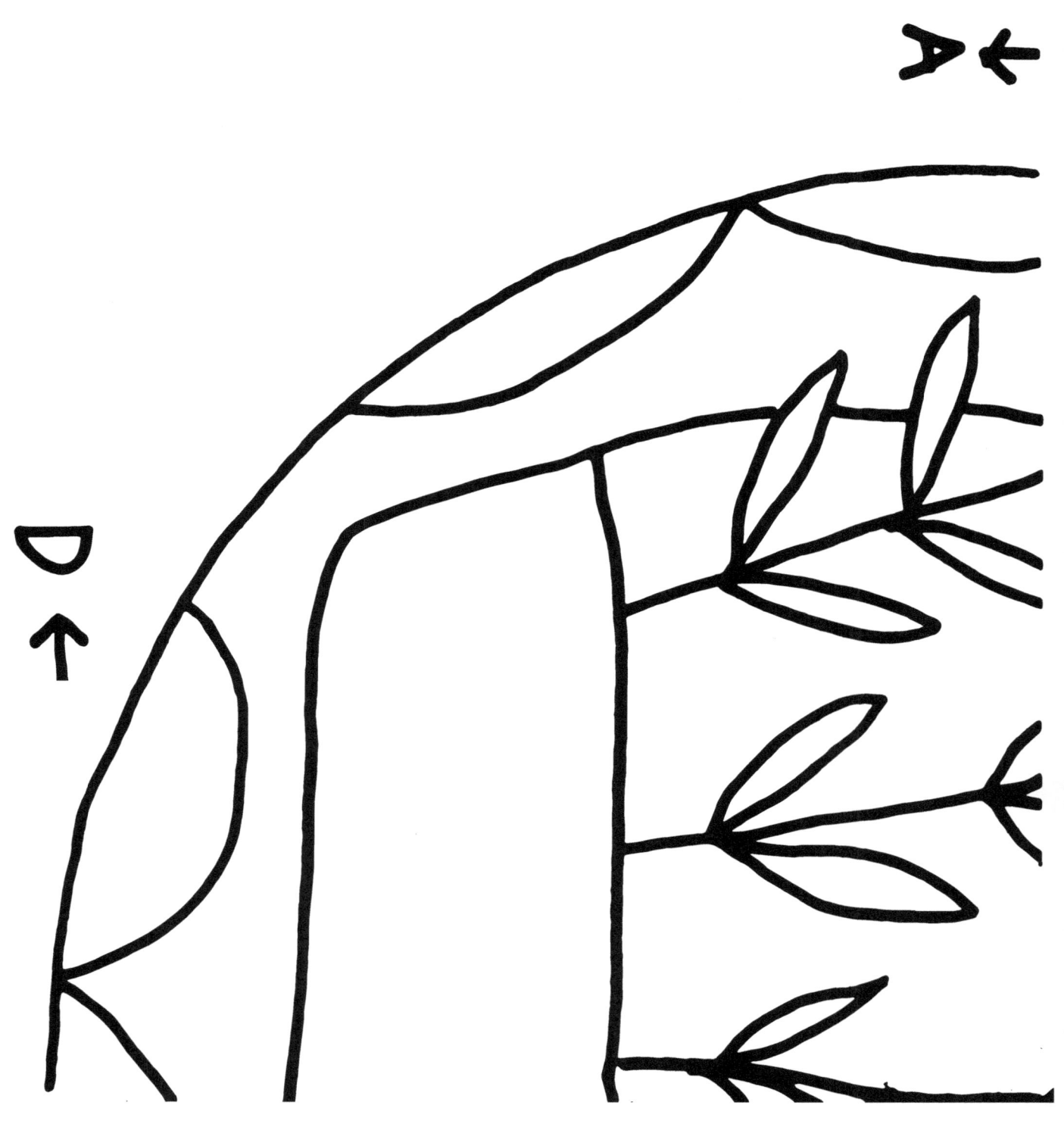

LAVENDER BASKET CHAIR PAD

43

LAVENDER BASKET CHAIR PAD

45

SIMPLE SEWING PROJECT

Cherry Tomato Pinkeep Necklace

Designed and Finished by Lori Brechlin

Finished Size: 2" × 1 ½" (not including the cord)

NEEDFULS

2 — 4" × 4" cotton fabric pieces of solid red (or use wool, flannel, etc.)

1 — 3" × 3" piece of green wool for leaves

Sawdust for stuffing

26" long piece of hemp cord or heavy crochet thread for necklace

Small white knitters ring

Sewing needle, cotton thread, small sharp scissors, pins, paper, pencil and chalk

INSTRUCTIONS

The template is on page 47.

Place 2 pieces of red fabric on your work surface, right sides together. Trace the cherry tomato template onto the white paper, and cut out on the line. Trace the outline of the paper template directly onto the wrong side of the top red fabric. Pin the pieces together.

Stitch completely around the entire circle by hand or machine using cotton thread. Trim away the excess fabric to within ¼" from the seam. Cut a small slit into the red fabric, being careful not to cut both pieces. Clip the edges, and turn the project right sides out. Stuff the tomato firmly with sawdust, and stitch slit closed using cotton thread.

Trace the leaves template onto paper, and cut out on the line. Place the template onto the green wool, and trace around the paper template with chalk. Cut out on the line. Pin the wool leaves shape on top of the stitched slit on the tomato, being careful to center it, and pin in place. Using cotton thread, make small whip stitches to attach the leaves to the tomato.

Attach a ring to the top of the tomato using cotton thread. Attach the hemp cord to the ring, and tie the ends together.

Now wear your cheery, little cherry tomato while you work, to help mind those stray pins!

SUMMER AT NOTFORGOTTEN FARM

CHERRY TOMATO PINKEEP NECKLACE

About the Author

I grew up in Connecticut, loving the smell of the woods and the smell of salt air. I loved to take long walks in the ancient cemeteries and study crumbling headstones, their hand carved artwork stirring something in my old soul.

I can remember visiting homes of friends and relatives and seeing old samplers, hooked rugs and sewing items lovingly displayed. I loved to visit my aunts' homes, which were decorated much like I decorate today — with things made by hand, from their heart, made with not much money, but with much love.

My mom's side of the family is Pennsylvania German, and I think I gain most of my inspiration for my work from there. My favorite colors are soot, bone white, moss and sage greens, oxblood red, dirty brown, yellow ochre and robin's egg blue.

I love to sit in our old farmhouse when it is raining and stitch something, listening to the melody of raindrops on our tin roof.

I have a fondness for old and worn things — leather children's shoes and clothing, fraying and tattered samplers under old wavy glass and rugs hooked from spent clothing, made to warm the floors of early farmhouse kitchens.

I collect scraps of fabrics, balls of twine and yellowing ironstone. I gravitate toward dusty books and ripped upholstery, seeing not their imperfections, but their unique ability to calm and relax me.

I am forever finding inspiration from antique needlework and from Mother Nature — and I love all animals.

I hope the designs in this book inspire you to make something that will fill your heart. I am always available by email at **not4got@aol.com** if you ever have any questions.

— *Lori Brechlin*

www.ingramcontent.com/pod-product-compliance
Lightning Source LLC
Chambersburg PA
CBHW061118170426
43199CB00026B/2956